FACT PACK
Ireland Guide

Irish Language Ireland

A guide and a sourcebook for those interested in the Irish Language.

If you want to know about Irish…
If you want to learn Irish…
to read Irish books…
to educate your children
through Irish…
to visit Irish-speaking areas of Ireland.

If you want to do any of those things,
or all of those things!
Whether you're Irish… or visiting…
Whether you haven't a word of Irish.
Or have lots of words, and want to use them more

*Seo é an leabhar duit!**

*Which means 'this is the book for you!'

Mini-Vocabulary
A flavour of the Irish language...

DAYS OF THE WEEK
Monday - *Dé Luain*
Tuesday. *Dé Máirt*
Wednesday - *Dé Céadaoin*
Thursday - *Déardaoin*
Friday - *Dé hAoine*
Saturday - *Dé Sathairn*
Sunday - *Dé Domhnaigh*

SALUTATIONS
Dia duit - Hello
Conas tá tú ? - How are you?
Cén Chaoi a bhfuil tú ? - How are you ?
Go raibh maith agat - Thank you
Tá an lá go breá - It's a fine day
Tá, buíochas le Dia - It is, thank God.

Fact Pack & Morrigan *are imprints of*
Morigna MediaCo Teo
Killala, County Mayo, Ireland
email: admin@atlanticisland.ie

©1998 Morigna MediaCo Teo

ISBN 0 907677 84 3

Origination by Morrigan
Printed in Ireland by Betaprint
Published in association with
Bord na Gaeilge *and* Údarás na Gaeltachta

Editors note:

I have drawn on many sources in compiling this information. The piece 'Irish Literature' on page 15 is largely based on extracts from a paper by Gearóid Denvir of UCG. Comhaltas Ceolteorí Eireann supplied the text for 'Irish Music' on page 16. 'Language Today' is based on information from the EU Bureau of Lesser Used Languages. 'Ancient Origins' is from a paper by the late Professor David Greene. The information on the Gaeltacht areas (including the maps) is based on that supplied by Udarás na Gaeltachta, with additional information from the Department of Arts, Culture and The Gaeltacht. The listings from page 21 onwards are largely based on those published by Bord na Gaeilge, who have also provided much input into the information contained in the general body of the publication.

Conan Kennedy.

Súil Eile

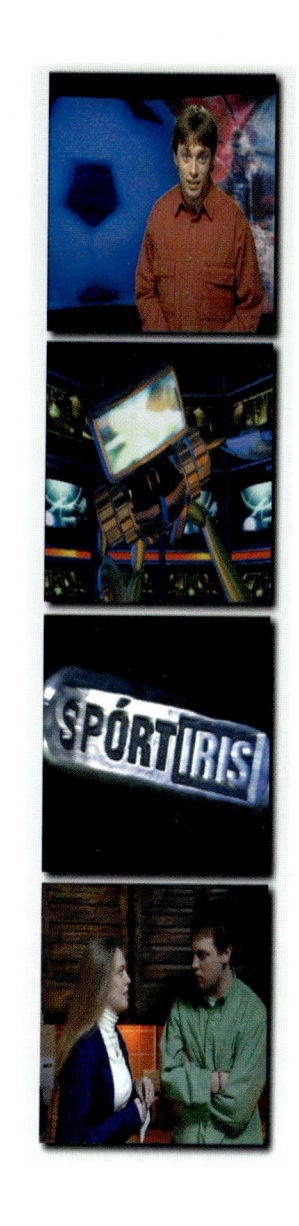

TnaG
Baile na hAbhann
Co. na Gaillimhe
Fón: 353 91 505050
Fax: 353 91 505021
E-mail: info@tnag.ie

TnaG

Cúrsaí Reatha, Nuacht, Spórt,

Cláracha agus scoth an Cheoil

ó 0800 go dtí 1930

gach lá den bhliain

FM 92-94 agus FM 102.7

ar fud na tíre.

Raidió na Gaeltachta
ar fud na tíre

GACH LÁ 0800 - 1930 ar 92 - 94FM agus 102.7FM

The Irish Language

Irish belongs to the Gaelic branch of Celtic, and is one of four original languages of Western Europe. It is also the oldest written vernacular in Europe. Irish is basically the same as the Gaelic of Scotland and is related to Welsh, to Breton and to ancient Gaulish. Irish was the common language of Ireland until the mid 19th century, but by the beginning of the 20th century its use as a vernacular was restricted to certain areas along the south, the west and north-west coasts. These areas, plus an enclave in the eastern part of the country in County Meath, are collectively known as

The Gaeltacht, *see page 18*

Active interest in the revival of Irish began at an academic level at the end of the 19th century. Douglas Hyde, later to become independent Ireland's first President, was one of those involved in the Gaelic League, a pioneering language organisation founded in 1843. During our own century vigorous efforts have been made by the Government, by State Agencies and by voluntary bodies to continue on with the work of language revival and the conservation of the Gaeltacht. Since 1922 Irish has been taught in all schools in the State. Throughout the country generally road signs are bilingual - (in the Gaeltacht areas they are in the Irish language only.) The national bus and train companies make extensive use of the Irish-language form of placenames and the visitor will notice the use of the language in many other places and situations.

Raidió na Gaeltachta and **Teílefís Na Gaeilge**
are the Irish-language broadcasting services from the Gaeltacht, *page 22*

Ancient Origins
The Scholarly perspective

"The Irish language derives from the Celtic branch of the proto-language conventionally labelled Indo-European; it is thus related to all the other languages of Europe with the exception of Basque, Estonian, Finnish and Hungarian, and its core vocabulary contains many words recognisable to speakers of other Indo-European languages, such as Dia 'God', má' thair 'mother', and rí, 'king'. The expansion of the Celtic-speaking peoples reached its peak around 500 BC and the succeeding centuries, and it was probably during that period that they reached Britain and Ireland. Celtic languages are dominant in both these islands when our historical evidence begins, and it is only these forms of Celtic which are known to us as written and spoken languages. The general term for them is Insular Celtic, divided into British (or Brythonic) and Irish (or Goidelic): some writers use the terms P Celtic and 0 Celtic respectively, based on the fact that British had the sound p (mapos 'son') where Irish had q (maqqos), though the modern reflexes are Welsh mab and Irish mac. Continental Celtic dialects never reached the status of fully written languages, and gradually died out during the early centuries of the Christian era, the best-known example of the process being the replacement of Gaulish Celtic by Latin, later to become French. Breton, which is a Celtic language still spoken on the European mainland, does not descend from Gaulish: as its name shows, it is a variety of British Celtic brought from Cornwall in south-west Britain by a movement of population resulting from the Anglo-Saxon invasions, which began in the 5th century AD, and which ultimately changed the dominant language of the island from British to English. The Cornish form of British itself died out in the 18th century. and Welsh is now the only form of British surviving in the island. The other Celtic language of Britain, Scottish Gaelic, is in fact an Irish dialect, deriving from population movements from Ireland to Scotland of roughly the same period as the Anglo-Saxon penetration of the south of the island: for most of the historical period Scotland has been linguistically divided between Irish and English, though these languages are more usually called (Scottish) Gaelic and Scots respectively. Another word for Scottish Gaelic is Erse, which is simply the Scots form of the word 'Irish,' Gaelic derives from Ga/dhl/g, the native name of the language. This in turn derives from Old Irish Go/deig, associated with Go/del 'Irishman', from which the technical term Go/del/c has been coined; Gaelic is a convenient term to cover both the Irish and Scottish dialects. as well as that of the Isle of Man, where Gaelic was established in pre-historic times, though if ceased to be spoken as a community language early in the present century. Up to the end of the 16th century, Gaelic-speaking Scotland used Irish as its literary language; after that a standard based on the local vernacular began to emerge, and Scottish Gaelic and Irish must now be regarded as separate languages, the relationship being roughly comparable to those existing between Danish and Swedish, or between Portuguese and Spanish".

The above is an extract from a paper by the late Professor David Greene, senior professor with

The School of Celtic Studies

The School of Celtic Studies is part of the Dublin Institute for Advanced Studies, a state body founded in 1940 at the behest of the then Taoiseach, Éamon de Valera. The two primary functions of the School are (1) to investigate and publish the manuscript materials which are extant in Irish, and to analyse and publish scientific descriptions of all varieties of the Irish language, written and spoken. (2) To act as publisher for works of scholarship on all aspects of Celtic Studies. The School's extensive list of publications is listed on their website, *http://www.dias.ie/celtic.html*

EXTANT: — STILL EXISTING

Languages today.

The existence of a language is usually a culture's most conspicuous distinguishing mark. Language is more than an assemblage of sounds, words and grammar. A language contains the collective memory of a community and is often associated with differences in social relationships, moral values, political outlook and traditions.

Within the EC there are more than 30 autochthonous or distinct languages in everyday use. Of these nine are official, working languages of the community: Danish, Dutch, English, French, German, Greek, Italian, Portuguese and Spanish. Irish is described as a 'treaty' language. Of the 320 million EC citizens, close to 50 million, or nearly one in six, speak a language other than the main or official language of the member state in which they live. These languages include some of the oldest in the western world, possessing rich cultural, literary, academic and folk traditions. Irish is, of course, among the most ancient of these, and perhaps the richest of all. And the others? Europe's linguistic patchwork is astonishing. In Denmark there is Danish and German. In France there is French, Catalan, Corsican and Occitan. Also German, a type of Dutch, Basque, and Breton. In Germany there is, in addition to German, both North and Saterland Frisian, Danish, and Polish. In Greece there is Greek, Arvinite, Aromanian, Slav and Turkish. In Italy there is Italian, French, Albanian, Catalan, Croatian, Franco Provençal, Friulan, Greek, Ladin, Occitan, Sardinian, Slovene and German. Netherlands has Dutch and Frisian. Luxembourg has Letzeburgesch and uses French whilst the written media is in German. Portugal has Portuguese. Spain has Spanish (Castillian) and Catalan, also Basque and Galician. United Kingdom has English, Scots Gaelic, Lallans, Cornish and Welsh. Sinti-Roma is spoken by the Gypsy people of Europe.

Language & Business

ADVERTISING: In several European countries, minority languages are being used successfully in the area of advertising. Occitan *(see previous page)* and Scots' Gaelic provide backdrops of image and atmosphere in French and English-language TV advertisements. In Spain, Catalan is also used extensively in TV advertising. In the context of Ireland, Irish has been used by car manufacturers, drinks companies and food producers. A leading advertiser says "Advertising is about communications and emotion. We live in a video culture and we tend to ignore language. As a result, the quality is becoming poorer. Now it's sound bites and pop speak. Irish can add potency to language by being unusual and because it taps so much emotion in its listeners. The benefits to advertisers are not just financial; it shows a breadth of vision when you advertise in Irish".

PRODUCTS: Many products use brand names in Irish, *Siúcra* sugar, *Fiacla* toothpaste, *Folláin* jam and *Solus* light bulbs are household names. Marketing people point out that surveys show that Irish people have a strong desire to buy local brands. And a key point is that Irishness can be defined in terms of the Irish language and not just the origin of the product.

Gnó le Gaeilge - Irish means business

This is an ongoing Bord na Gaeilge *(see page 21)* project which makes practical suggestions to businesses and helps identify opportuunities for applying bilingualism. (A translation service is available). The project assesses the many ways in which businesses, large and small, can incorporate Irish in their activities, in signage, spoken Irish with customers, business identification and in marketing and public relations.

Public Signs - Community Projects

A minority language is extremely valuable in creating a 'sense of place'. This 'sense' is not only important for residents' feeling of well-being, but it enhances the experience of visitors. (This latter fact is strongly recognised by the Welsh Tourist Board/Bwrd Croeso Cymru which actively seeks to promote the Welsh language in tourist amenities). Currently in Ireland many major retailers use Irish in a proportion of their branches, these including Dunnes Stores, Tesco/Crazy Prices, Superquinn, Super Valu, The Body Shop, Iceland and Waterstones.

Projects are being set up in various centres to increase the use of Irish language signage in public areas. These centres include Cork, Carlow, Nenagh and Athy and are based on the successful 'Gaillimh le Gaeilge' project in Galway City. Set up in 1987 with the support of Galway Chamber of Commerce and under the management of Comhdáil Náisiúnta na Gaeilge, the project has achieved much. Today, practically all Galway streets have a number of businesses featuring Irish-only and bilingual signs. All city supermarkets carry bilingual signage, and bilingualism also extends to the public address system. Many hotels and restaurants also feature Irish on their menus.

Tidy Towns

The Irish language forms part of this competition's criteria under various categories.

Placenames Commission

This Commission was appointed by the Government in 1946 to 'ascertain the correct Irish forms of the placenames of Ireland, and to compile them...' Later, a special section of the Ordnance Survey was created, The Placenames Branch, to carry out this work. Currently its main duty is to service the mapping work of the Ordnance Survey, and the Branch also provides services to Government Departments and State Agencies such as OPW, Bord Fáilte, CIE, Local Authorities and so forth. The Placenames Branch is based at the Ordnance Survey Office in Dublin's Phoenix Park.

(See also page 14)

Facts & Figures

- A January '97 survey (*IMS, commissioned by BnaG*) found that 65% of respondents felt that "Irish is a vital part of our culture. Every reasonable step should be taken to ensure it remains a language of everyday use".

- The number of all-Irish schools, Gaelscoileanna, *(see page 12)* outside of Gaeltacht areas has increased to 140 (January 1998 figure).

- There has been a big increase in the number of adults attending Irish classes.

- Eight out of ten adults *(recent IMS survey)* felt that bilingual signs in everyday locations are a good idea.

- According to the latest census figures released (1991), 32.5% of the population, or 1,095,830 people recorded themselves as having knowledge of Irish.

- There is an even distribution of Irish speakers throughout the country, not just in Gaeltacht areas.

- According to the 1996 Census of Population the total Gaeltacht population is 83,000. Of the total workforce of 28,500 some 7,900 people are now in full time employment while an additional 4,000 are seasonally employed in the broad variety of enterprises assisted by Údarás na Gaeltachta *(see page 35)*. These enterprises include electronics, aquaculture (finfish and shellfish), engineering, textiles, fish processing, audio-visual and tourism.

Education through Irish

Obviously in the Gaeltacht the schools are conducted mainly in Irish but increasingly in recent years, Irish-medium schools are being set up outside the Gaeltacht where children (generally from English-speaking homes) receive all their education through the medium of Irish. A whole new generation of Irish-speaking children is emerging and, in combination with the ongoing work of **Bord na Gaeilge** *(page 21),* **Údarás na Gaeltachta** *(pages 18 & 35)*and other agencies, there is renewed hope for the future of our native language. The organisation concerned with the development of Irish-medium schools outside of the Gaeltacht is **Gaelscoileanna** *(see page 12).*

Visiting the Gaeltacht

The modern Gaeltacht population is bi-lingual in Irish and English so the visitor will have no difficulty in being understood. There are several phrase books available for visitors who wish to try basic Irish - these are also useful in understanding the meaning of place names. These names can tell a lot about the history and background of particular locations. For many years there have been summer residential courses in Gaeltacht areas for children from English-speaking homes, and now over 24,000 young people participate in Gaeltacht summer courses each year. More recently courses for adults have been initiated in several areas. These deal with, in addition to the language, many aspects of Irish culture and environment.
Gaeltacht-based Irish Courses for Adults,
(see page 31)

GaelSaoire,
Holidays in the Gaeltacht,
Freephone 1800 621 600.

Comhdháil Náisiúnta na Gaeilge

is the federation of major non-statutory Irish language organisations. It receives State funding and employs full-time staff.

Comhdháil Náisiúnta na Gaeilge
46 Sráid Chill Dara, Baile Átha Cliath 2.
Guthán (01)6794780.

Irish-medium Schools

Irish-medium schools are primary schools and post-primary schools functioning in accordance with the usual rules of the Department of Education. Irish is the language of instruction in these schools and the language of communication amongst teachers, children and management. A high educational standard exists in all subjects, including English, and the usual programme set out by the Department of Education is followed. Irish is the living language of Irish-medium schools, both within the classroom and without. At present there are 114 Irish medium primary schools and 26 Irish medium secondary schools outside of the Gaeltacht. *(See* **Gaelscoileanna,** *following page).*

In addition to the primary and secondary schools there are 276 naíonra (pre-schools) in operation at present. The organisation for promoting and supporting Irish language pre-school groups is

An Comhchoiste Réamhscoláíochta Teo.,
7 Cearnóg Mhuirfean,
Baile Átha Cliath 2.
Guthán (01) 6763222

This organisation receives State funding and, employing full-time staff, provides training and publication of resource material for pre-schools.

Gaelscoileanna

A voluntary national organisation, established in 1973, which assists Irish-medium schools to overcome difficulties and to support their development. Gaelscoileanna provides information, help, support and advice to parents who wish to establish Irish-medium schools or to develop a school as an Irish-medium school. Gaelscoileanna acts as an intermediary between Irish-medium schools and The Department of Education and meets the Department regularly to discuss matters relating to Irish-medium education. Gaelscoileanna organises training courses for Boards of Management and teachers. Gaelscoileanna arranges conferences on subjects relating to Irish-medium education. Gaelscoileanna also supports Irish-medium schools in organising joint events. A magazine is published by Gaelscoileanna twice a year.

Gaelscoileanna,
7 Merrion Square, Dublin 2.
Phone (01) 6763222

Irish in Education

In the mainstream English language education system the position in relation to Irish language is as follows:

PRIMARY LEVEL:
Irish is taught in all schools.

SECONDARY LEVEL:
All students in State funded schools are required to study Irish as a school subject. There is a percentage marking advantage when doing exams through Irish.

THIRD LEVEL:
The National University of Ireland requires all candidates to have passed the Leaving Certificate paper in Irish.

Studying Irish at Third Level:

Irish is taught in all universities and some other third level colleges.

Studying *through* Irish at Third Level:

University College Galway
Some degree courses are taught through the medium of Irish. Other courses taught through Irish include *Diploma in Applied Communications*

Dublin City University
B.Sc in Finance, Computing and Enterprise

Careers and Irish

PRIMARY TEACHING COURSES
Applications for a training place in one of the five colleges of education are now made through the CAO system. The five colleges are Mary Immaculate Limerick; and in Dublin the following: St Patrick's College, Drumcondra; Coláiste Mhuire, Marino; Church of Ireland College of Education, Rathmines; Froebel College of Education, Blackrock.

The minimum entry requirements include for Grade C3 in the Leaving Certificate Higher Level Paper in Irish.

THE PUBLIC SERVICE
Fluency and ability in Irish have always been regarded as advantageous in the public service, provided they co-exist with professional qualifications and personal skills. Government policy states that every citizen has the right to conduct business with the public service through Irish.

CHOICE SHOULD ALSO BE A RIGHT!!

Further Information:
Gairmeacha le Gaeilge/Careers With Irish, (Bord na Gaeilge, 1996), Ciarán MacMurchaidh agus Rhoda O'Connor.

Place Names

The great majority of Irish place names are derived from the Irish language. Words associated with natural features, ancient structures, gods and people, battles and events, all are found as the roots or prefixes to our placenames. In these names we will find rivers, fords, lakes, mountains and plains, forts and castles, all the records of past ages. There are many thousand of these words, but some of the most common, ones that appear repeatedly, are amongst the following:

Bally...from an Irish word that originally merely described a 'place', later came to mean 'town'.
Borris...not strictly from the Irish language, but borrowed therein from the anglo-Norman 'Borough'.
Brugh, also **Bru**...the original word meant a 'palace' or 'distinguished residence'.
Caiseal, also **Cashel**...words deriving from that for 'a circular stone fort'.
Carn...a pile of stones, either marking a grave or a place of sudden death.
Cathair, Caher, Cahir...similar meanings to above, but also later coming to mean 'a city'.
Cill, also as **Kill, Kil, Kyle, Keel** and **Cal**...generally from the word for 'church', though a proportion from another word meaning 'woods'.
Dun, Doon...a fort, particularly one that was a royal residence.
Grianan, Greenan, Greenoge...a sunny spot, though generally related to a fort in a sunny spot.
Lios, Liss...a circular mound or trench around a dwelling, either as fortification or shelter.
※ **Moat**...borrowed from the English language, the Irish version meaning a large high mound rather than water filled ditch.
Rath...similar to Lios above.
Ros...a wood.
Tara...elevated spot with good view.
Tin, Tinna...from the word for house.

※ FROM OXFORD DICTIONARY.
MOAT. DEFENSIVE DITCH ROUND A CASTLE ETC. USUALLY FILLED WITH WATER.

Literature in Irish

The oldest written literature of Europe is in the Irish language. Even before the coming of Christianity to Ireland in the 5th Century, Ireland had a flourishing and highly developed oral culture of immense antiquity, and it was this culture that was carried forward with the advent of writing. 'Writing' was introduced to Ireland by Christian monks, using Latin at first, but becoming gaelicized and writing in Irish from the end of the 6th Century onwards. From that time on there was an unbroken tradion of writing for a thousand years until the collapse of the Gaelic order in the 17th Century. This writing preserved much folklore, mythology and proto history from the earliest of times, a body of information which significantly influenced the 'celtic revival' and inevitably led to the political movements which brought about the modern Ireland. **Conradh na Gaeilge** *(see page 24)* was founded in 1893 with one of its aims the production of a modern literature in Irish. This was not before its time, as at that date there were only about five Irish language books in print!

Major Irish-language writers of this century include Máirtín Ó Cadhain (1905-1970), Seán Ó Ríordáin (1917-1977) and Máirtín Ó Direáin (1910-1988). More recently the novelist Séamas Mac Annaidh and the poet Nuala Ní Dhomhnaill have established international reputations. Publishing in Irish today is not, however, confined to 'high' literature. Easy to read novels by writers such as Breandán Ó hEithir and Páraig Standún have been on best seller lists, and a whole range of publications, from books for children and teenagers to books on sport, history, religion, local lore, biography, cookery and other special interest areas, is readily available. There are also numerous bilingual prose and poetry publications.

The major Irish language book distributor is
ÁIS *(see page 27)*

Traditional Music

Traditional or 'folk' music has a high profile in modern Ireland for several reasons. The Industrial Revolution here did not take the same form as in many other countries. Music did not become smothered by the new culture. And, more particularly perhaps, the Irish have always been a people with a strong love of music, dance, story-telling, getting together.
This music was played at all gatherings, and especially at local level in someone's house in the countryside where neighbours would gather to play cards, sing, dance and tell stories. Special nights or scoraiocht would be held, larger groups of people coming together in halls or barns. Musicians from far and wide were welcome at these and there were, in fact, many professional travelling musicians who sang and played at markets and fairs, bringing tunes and songs from one area to another, teaching the skills to young people.
The major cities in Ireland, and then in Britain and the USA, became part of this intermingling of musicians, immigrants and young people. The music lived on.
The period from the '60s on has seen great vigour, strength and excitement in the story of Irish music, despite difficult times in the 30's and 40's. Of course the music has changed in style and presentation, bringing it more in harmony with the modern lifestyles of the people, with the venues in which it is played and with its presence on radio and television. But it is still very much the essential music of Ireland. Of old Ireland, and new Ireland alike.

Irish traditional music comes in two forms, vocal and instrumental. The latter is mostly dance music - reels, jigs, hornpipes, polkas, set-dances, mazurkas - the remainder being marches, slow airs (usually song tunes) and 'planxties', which are harpers' pieces surviving from the 17th or 18th centuries. Tunes have various origins, but it is possible to state generally that they were mostly composed in the 18th and 19th centuries, that they were passed down aurally through generations of music makers and that practitioners of the art of traditional music share a common approach and set of techniques in their interpretation of this music. Within this common approach individual musicians interpret, rework and refurbish the old tunes, through the use of various forms of ornamentation and of melodic and rhythymic variation. These variations and ornamentations are generally minor ones, involving just a few notes in a particular phase of a tune, yet when executed with skill and subtlety they can show a considerable level of imagination and even creativity.

Traditional songs in Ireland include the old songs in Irish which may be heard in the Gaeltacht areas along the western coast, and which are sung in what is called the sean nós or 'old style'; and songs in the English language (but with an Irish character or flavour) of which there are numerous examples in various regional and personal styles.

Of the instruments normally used in playing Irish traditional music the only uniquely Irish instrument is the uilleann pipes, so-called because they are blown by a bellows under the arm and elbow, ulleann being the Irish-language word for elbow. The fiddle, the two-row accordion, the wooden concert flute and the tin whistle will be found to the fore in any big session, and the banjo too is very popular. The concertina, piano accordion and mandolin are less widely played, except for Co.Clare where the concertina is very popular. The harp was once Ireland's foremost musical instrument, and has seen a revival in recent years. The guitar, the bouzouki and the piano are the instruments mostly used for accompaniment. The bodhran, a simple hand-held goatskin drum, is widely used, and one may also find the rhythms being tapped out with a pair of bones or spoons. Drums are usually used in ceili bands.

Údarás na Gaeltachta
The Regional Development Authority

The Gaeltacht
Ireland at its most Irish!

A culture stands apart because of its view of itself and the world. In the Gaeltacht, Irish culture can be experienced in a completely different way to elsewhere in Ireland. The reason for this is that in the Gaeltacht, the Irish language is still spoken on a community basis.

Those who speak Irish today are continuing an unbroken tradition that stretches back, in its current form, to at least the 9th century. The modes of thinking, the rhythms and the world view contained in the language retain an independence that has survived centuries of oppression, a campaign of mass Anglicisation and the more recent global assault by dominant western media.

Because of the history of the country, the oral tradition has played an extremely important role in the continuation of Irish. Poetry, song and narrative prose carried the exploits of heroes, kings, queens and mythical figures across the generations.

There is much research and debate on the exact origins of the Irish language, but it is generally believed that it is one of several Celtic languages that belong to the Indo-European family. The Irish language is one of the oldest written languages. Inscriptions engraved in Ogham on standing stones date back to the 6th century AD. Latin manuscripts from the 7th-9th century define the grammar for Old Irish and legal texts written in Old Irish survive from the 7th and 8th centuries.

The Gaeltacht - A feast of many dishes

Of course culture is a feast of many dishes. Music, song, storytelling, dancing, archaeology, mythology, history, language, names, place-names - as well as place - all combine to colour the experience for the visitor. Irish language schools offer a range of courses, at various levels, for those who want to be initiated into the magic of the language as well as those who want to develop their fluency.

There is an increasing trend of Irish people coming to the Gaeltacht to study the language as a means of defining their Irishness, as a way of increasing their understanding of their unique identity. People from abroad come too - to experience a language and people rich in poetry, music and fun. A certain buzz can be created from communicating in a variety of settings: in the pub, at a ceili or out on a sports field. Many visitors treasure the opportunity of sharing and participating in local activities such as marts and horse fairs, or religious and secular festivals and celebrations. The pursuit of the elusive 'craic' or merriment has brightened up many a life and can result in people losing their hearts - if not their souls - to this magical language and place.

The Gaeltacht - A sense of place

The Gaeltacht can be a place the visitor passes through, in awe of its breathtaking scenery, or it can be a place to visit in itself, for itself. A store abounds of ancient sites, buildings and items of archaeological interest dating back to the earliest known races of people on this island. There is much to be explored, within the local communities or in the newly-built interpretative centres that can be used as a passport to the experience of place.The history and lifestyles of centuries of Irish lives can be gathered, for example, at the Ceide Fields, in Co Mayo; at Ionad an Bhlascaoid, in Dún Chaoin or Ionad Árainn, on the Aran Islands.

The Gaeltacht - Environment

It is hard to separate a people from their language or a language from its environment. An interesting route to the Irish-speaking world is through an exploration of Irish place and family names. For the urban dweller of today it can be hard to imagine a time when each small area, often no bigger than a field, had its own name, giving information of significance and often a sense of its history. The Irish landscape is dotted with names that evoke a people whose customs and habits respected and were at ease with their environment. And as with place-names, so also with people's names. Both surnames and first names can be traced back to locations, events and people that are mentioned in the earliest records that are available.

The natural environment of the Gaeltacht is very varied. Some regions are carpeted in bog, some are of rolling hills, some are of mountain ranges, while others are by lakes or the ocean. Each has its own special magic on offer; all combined offer a rare treat. Painters, potters, designers, knitters, visual and musical artists, film-makers, writers and scores of other people have found inspiration for their work in the Gaeltacht landscape.

On visiting the Gaeltacht, the organic relationship between the person and the natural environment can be easily understood. For centuries people have lived and worked in these environments at fishing, farming, weaving, spinning and a host of other traditional crafts and trades. Their handiwork such as Donegal tweed, Aran sweaters, traditional musical instruments and native boats is known and loved world-wide.

page 35 contains further information on
Údarás na Gaeltachta
A pull-out map of the Gaeltacht regions is inside back cover.

BORD NA GAEILGE

Easy Ways To Make More Of Your Irish

Now that you have decided to use your Irish or brush up on it, the listings overleaf are intended to guide you towards your next step. That could be to learn simple greetings, read signs and understand placenames, to follow radio and television programmes or to speak the language fluently and become part of the growing Irish-speaking community - the choice is yours! The important thing is to decide what best suits you and to act accordingly. Be patient with yourself as any course of learning takes both time and effort.

We wish you every success.

Go n-éirí go geal leat!

Micheál Ó Muircheartaigh
Cathaoirleach

BORD NA GAEILGE
7 Cearnóg Mhuirfean, Baile Átha Cliath 2
7 Merrion Square, Dublin 2.

Guthán/*Phone* (01) 676 3222, 1850-325-325
Facs/*FAX* (01)661 6564

Ríomhphost/*Email: bng@iol.ie*
An tIdirlíon/*Internet: http://www.BnaG.ie*

Irish and the Broadcast Media

A useful way to keep in regular contact with the language is to watch programmes on television and listen to radio programmes in Irish. This is particularly helpful when done in conjunction with an Irish course in a group or individual setting.

Television:
There are several television programmes on both RTÉ1 and Network 2. Programmes in Irish are occasionally broadcast on BBC and UTV. Programme schedules appear in the RTÉ Guide, and in the press.

Teilifís na Gaeilge
Teilifís na Gaeilge is available nationwide and its schedule caters for a broad range of interests ranging from *'Ros na Rún'* (daily drama series) to news, sport, music and light entertainment.
Programmes are sub-titled in English on *Aertel.*

Teletext
Gaeltext, an Irish language information service is available on Aertel, RTÉ's teletext service. Information on Irish courses and conversation groups is a feature of the service. To avail of *Gaeltext* press number 480 while tuned to Network 2. Further information at (01) 491 0252

Radio:

RTÉ Radio 1 and 2FM

RTÉ Radio 1 broadcasts Nuacht and a variety of programmes in Irish in its schedules. News headlines in Irish are broadcast on 2FM.
See RTÉ Guide and press for programme information.

Raidió na Gaeltachta

Available nationwide on FM, Raidió na Gaeltachta broadcasts daily from 8.00 am. to 7.30 pm.
See RTÉ Guide and press for programme information.

Raidió na Life

Broadcasting on 102.2 FM, this is an Irish language community station based in Dublin.

A number of local radio stations broadcast programmes in Irish as part of their schedules; this is particularly so in the case of community stations. Check your local newspaper for details

Courses and Conversation Circles

Courses and/or conversation circles are often organised locally by Irish language organisations, schools, naíonraí, cultural or sporting organisation as well as by interested individuals. For details check local press and radio, community noticeboards, Gaeltext (Aertel)., or enquire from the local branches of Irish/cultural organisations.

AN BRADÁN FEASA is an information service about the Irish language, including events, organisations and services:
An Bradán Feasa,
45, Dominic Street, Galway.
Phone: (091) 567 824/565 139 Fax: (091) 563 699
Email: conradh@bradan.iol.ie

Principal Course Providers

Adult Education Organisers
Adult Education Organisers are employed by Vocational Education Committees to organise adult education provision in their area. In most cases a course or conversation circle will be set up if there is sufficient demand; your local adult education office will be able to advise you.

Conradh na Gaeilge
This organisation has branches and clubs throughout the country, many of which organise courses and conversation groups.
Conradh na Gaeilge,
6, Harcourt Street, Dublin, 2. Phone 01 - 475 7401

Gael Linn/Foras na Gaeilge
Gael Linn is a national foundation which has the strengthening and spreading of the Irish language as its main aim. Its subsidiary, Foras na Gaeilge, organises intensive Irish courses, principally at Gael Linn's head office, and in the Donegal Gaeltacht.
Gael Linn/Foras na Gaeilge,
26-27 Merrion Square, Dublin 2. Phone 01- 676 7283

Glór na nGael
This is an annual competition to ascertain which community has made the best effort to stimulate and spread the use of Irish locally. A local committee made up of language and cultural organisations and other interested people comes together to organise courses, conversation groups and other activities which are intended to make the Irish more a part of community life. Some 140 local committees are to be found throughout the country.
Glór na nGael,
46, Kildare Street, Dublin 2. Phone 01-679 4780

Self-Instructional Courses

Audio Cassette Courses:

NOW YOU'RE TALKING *(Gill & Macmillan)*
Based on the popular television series which was shown on BBC/RTÉ, this course makes extensive use of the Ulster dialect.

BASIC IRISH FOR PARENTS *(An Comhchoiste Réamhscolaíochta)*
This course was designed to help parents of children attending naíonraí, and has since proven very popular with parents generally. The package consists of a book and a single audio cassette which is available in each of the three main dialects, Connacht, Munster and Ulster and also in the standardised dialect.

BUNTÚS CAINTE *(An Gúm/Gael Linn)*
First broadcast as a television series in the early days of Teilifís Éireann, it is still hugely popular, and is available in book and cassette.

COGAR *(Gael Linn)*
Originally broadcast as a radio series, this course is now available on four cassettes and an instructional booklet.

CÚRSA CLOSAMHAIRC *(Ogmios)*
A self-instructional course for adults produced in the Ulster dialect.

LEARNING IRISH, Mícheál Ó Siadhail. *(Yale University Press)*
This course which would suit the student with an academic background is based on the Connemara (Cois Fharraige) dialect.

TEACH YOURSELF IRISH, Diarmuid Ó Sé/Joseph Shiels. *(Hodder & Stoughton.)*
The aim of this course is to teach one to understand basic, everyday Irish. It is suitable both for the complete beginner and for people who learned some Irish at school, but who have had little opportunity of speaking it. It is accompanied by a pronunciation guide on a single cassette. Revised and updated in 1994.

IRISH FOR BEGINNERS *(Usborne)*
This short course for beginners is very basic and is intended to teach the Irish one would find useful in everyday situations.

LINGUAPHONE IRISH COURSE
Part of a best-selling series worldwide, this course comprises four cassettes and a book.
Widely available in libraries, this course may be ordered from The Linguaphone Institute, 41 Upper Liffey Street, Dublin 1.

Courses in Book Form:

IRISH PHRASE BOOK/RÁ LEABHAR *(Mercier Press/Bord na Gaeilge)*
This book is intended to help people conduct simple conversations in Irish.

IRISH IS FUN & IRISH IS FUNTASTIC *(Y Lolfa)*
A two-part basic Irish conversation course which makes extensive use of cartoons. Its approach is both humourous and unconventional.

THE LAZY WAY TO IRISH *(Y Lolfa)*
This book is intended for someone interested in making a start, before proceeding to a more conventional course.

Irish and The Printed Word

There is a range of publications available in Irish, ranging from books to periodicals and weekly newspapers.

Books

Some 100 books in Irish are published annually and they comprise light fiction, poetry, prose and educational books. The subject matter is wide and there are books which cater for children, teenagers and adults. Some works are published in bilingual format. Your local bookseller can order any book you require from Áis, Bord na Gaeilge's book distribution agency. Bord na Gaeilge also produces *An Léitheoir,* a quarterly bilingual newsletter detailing new publications in Irish.

Your local library stocks a range of Irish language books. If you require a book which is not in stock you can request it through your library for a nominal charge. An increasing number of libraries now have self-instructional courses available for use at the library. It is advisable to book these facilities, as they tend to be in great demand. Ask your local librarian for details .

Newspapers & Periodicals

FOINSE
the weekly newspaper, is available nationwide.

LÁ
the Belfast-based weekly newspaper may be ordered from:
Lá, Cultúrlann Mac Adam-Ó Fiaich, Bóthar na bhFál, Béal Feirste. Phone (0801232) 239303.

COMHAR
This monthly magazine covers current affairs,
language and social issues, literature and poetry.
Comhar Teo., 5, Merrion Row, Dublin, 2
Phone/Fax: (01) 678 5443

FEASTA
This monthly magazine is published by Conradh na
Gaeilge and is available from its head office:
Feasta, 6, Sráid Fhearcrair, Baile Átha Cliath, 2.
Phone (01) 475 7401.

MAHOGANY GASPIPE
This teenage magazine produced by Bord na Gaeilge,
is available three times annually.
Mahogany Gaspipe, 7 Merrion Square, Dublin, 2
Phone (01) 676 3222

AN SAGART
This quarterly religious magazine is available from:
An Sagart, Marianella, 75, Bóthar Orwell, Baile Átha
Cliath, 6.   Phone 628 5222

AN TIMIRE
This quarterly religious magazine is available from:
An Timire, Páirc Bhaile an Mhuilinn, Baile Átha
Cliath, 6   Phone (01) 269 8411

SAOL
A free monthly newsletter (subject to postal charge).
Saol, 7 Merrion Square, Dublin, 2
Phone (01) 676 3222

AN tULTACH
Comhaltas Uladh produces this monthly magazine.
An Rúnaí, An tUltach, 2, Orpheus Drive, Dungannon,
Co. Tyrone. (0801232) 612707

Dictionaries :

AN FOCLÓIR PÓCA. *(An Gúm)*
Irish-English/English-Irish
This pocket dictionary was first printed in 1986, with the aim of meeting the needs of school-goers and of the general public. It comprises a wide and useful modern vocabulary in both Irish and English as well as a good sprinkling of exemplary phrases.

ENGLISH-IRISH DICTIONARY, De Bhaldraithe *(An Gúm)*
First published in 1959 this is still the standard English-Irish reference dictionary.

FOCLÓIR GAEILGE-BÉARLA, Ó Dónaill *(An Gúm)*
First printed in 1972, this is the standard Irish-English reference dictionary. This is a general standardised dictionary which covers the more common aspects of today's Irish language usage. It features contemporary language as used in the Gaeltacht, the language of literature and new terminology.

GEARRFHOCLÓIR Ó DÓNAILL *(An Gúm)*
This is a shortened version of the standard Irish-English reference dictionary referred to above.

Basic Grammars:

NEW IRISH GRAMMAR
New Irish Grammar has been designed for students who feel the need of a single compact Irish grammar in English.

IRISH GRAMMAR - A BASIC HANDBOOK
The aim of this book is to provide a basic working and reference grammar of the Irish language in English.

Audio Cassettes

A number of cassettes and compact discs of music and the spoken word in Irish suitable for both young and old are available from good record stores. In case you have difficulty, or if you would like a catalogue, the principal suppliers are
Cló Iar-Chonnachta Teo., Teach Mór, Indreabhán, Co. na Gaillimhe. Phone: (091) 593307
Gael-Linn Teo., 25 Merrion Square, Dublin 2.
Phone: (01) 676 7283

Video

In recent times a number of cartoon videos in Irish have come on stream. These are available from Telegael and from RTÉ Enterprises. Gael-Linn have also produced some archive videos which are well worth checking out.

MUZZY
Cartoon-based Irish courses for children, produced by Telegael for use mainly in schools.
Telegael, An Spidéal, Co. na Gaillimhe,
Phone (091) 553460

WHO SAID THAT?
This and other learning aids for school use are available from
Comhar na Múinteoirí Gaeilge, 7 Merrion Square, Dublin 2.

Computer Software

Everson Gunn Teoranta will design, host and revise Internet web pages for the Irish speaking community. They also write computer software.
Everson-Gunn Teoranta, 15, Camden Row, Dublin,
Phone: (01) 478 2597

Gaeltacht-Based Irish Courses for Adults

Gaeltacht-based courses for adults represent another option for improving your Irish. Most of these operate during the summer months, but an increasing number offer courses at other times of the year, eg., long weekends.

Co. Donegal - Gweedore

AN CHRANNÓG
Courses in conversational Irish with special emphasis on the Ulster dialect are offered on three levels depending on fluency already attained.
An Chrannóg, Na Doirí Beaga, Leitir Ceanainn, Co. Dhún na nGall
Phone 075 - 32188, Fax 075 - 32189

GAEL LINN/FORAS NA GAEILGE
Foras na Gaeilge organises intensive Irish courses in the Donegal Gaeltacht at Gweedore.
Gael Linn/Foras na Gaeilge, 26-27 Merrion Square, Dublin, 2 Phone 01 - 676 7283, Fax 01- 676 7030

Co. Donegal - Glencolumbkille and Glenfin

OIDEAS GAEL
The annual programme of courses and events brings together people from Ireland and abroad to participate in Gaeltacht life, improve their fluency in Irish and enjoy our living culture.
Oideas Gael, Gleann Cholmcille, Co. Dhún na nGall.
Phone/Fax 075 - 30248

Co. Galway - Carraroe

ÁRAS MHÁIRTÍN UÍ CHADHAIN
One and two week intensive courses in spoken Irish for adults. The teaching programme enables the learner to master basic structures, to improve fluency and accuracy and to build vocabulary.
Áras Mháirtín Uí Chadhain, An Ceathrú Rua, Co. na Gaillimhe. Phone 091 - 9510/595120, Fax 091- 59504. Email: mrbharry@iol.ie

Co. Galway - Aran Islands

OIDHREACHT OILEÁIN
The Irish-speaking island of Inisheer offers a unique opportunity to learners to become immersed in the language. An introduction to local history, singing and dancing form an integral part of this course.
Siarlinn Teo, Inis Oirr, Oileáin Árann, Co. na Gaillimhe. Phone (099) 75052

Co. Kerry

OIDHREACHT CHORCA DHUIBHNE
Founded as a subsidiary to Comharchumann Chorca Dhuibhne to draw attention to our heritage - language, history, geology, biology etc., and to preserve and develop it. *Oidhreacht Chorca Dhuibhne, Baile an Fhirtéaraigh, Trá Lí, Co. Chiarraí. Phone (066)56100, Fax (066) 56348*

Co. Meath
COLÁISTE EOGHAIN UÍ GHRAMHNAIGH
Providing courses in Irish at all levels.
Coláiste Eoghain Uí Ghramhnaigh, Ráth Cairn, Co. na Mí. Phone 046 - 32067

Using Your Irish

Summer Colleges
Most Irish people are familiar with the Irish courses in the Gaeltacht for children, teenagers and young adults. For further information, contact the co-ordinating body for organisers of the Summer Colleges.
An Rúnaí, CONCOS, 46, Kildare Street, Dublin, 2
Phone 01 - 679 4780

Festivals and Events:
There are numerous festivals and events where the Irish language plays a central role, and it is worth your while going to one or more of them to practice your Irish.

Éigsí
A number of weekend *Éigsí* or cultural festivals are organised throughout the country. Information from :
An Rúnaí, Comhdháil Náisiúnta na Gaeilge, 46, Kildare Street, Dublin 2.

An tOireachtas
This annual week-long event is the principal gathering of Irish speakers and organisations. In recent years, Bord na Gaeilge has organised events geared towards adult learners of Irish.
An tOireachtas, 6, Harcourt Street, Dublin 2.
Phone (01) 475 3857/475 7401

Cumann Merriman
Cumann Merriman organises a winter and a summer school each year. The Winter school is conducted through Irish. Contact can be made with:
An Rúnaí, Cumann Merriman, c/o Irish Department, University College Dublin, Belfield, Dublin, 4.
Phone (01) 679 4780

Internet & CD ROM

The Internet has become a popular way of communicating to the world, and the Irish language is well represented. (**Líonta Teo** provides Internet courses in Irish, and Bord na Gaeilge is helping them to develop plans to teach Irish on the Internet).

BORD NA GAEILGE
web pages are at *http://www.BnaG.ie*, here you can find information about the Bord itself and also links to a wide variety of online Irish language resources.

AN GRÉASÁN
Irish-language internet open access 'chatline' on the *Atlantic Island* internet system. Here in real time you can 'converse' with people around the world through Irish. *http://cgi-bin.iol.ie/cgi-bin/atlanticg.pl*

GAELIC-L
Set up in 1989 to bring Gaelic speakers from far and wide together on-line, at *http://www.smo.uhi.ac.uk/* To register as a member of this on-line Gaeltacht all one needs do is to send the order: SUBSCRIBE GAELIC-L, together with your name and surname to *listserve@listserve.hea*

EVERSON GUNN TEO
design, host and revise internet web pages for the Irish speaking community. Their web pages can be accessed at *http://www.indigo.ie/egt/*

SPEAKWRITE GAEILGE
Irish language course on CD ROM
GalMac Computers, Liosbaun Est.,Tuam Rd.,Galway.
email:mlbharry@iol.ie

LEARN IRISH (EUROTALK)
Basic Irish course on CD ROM.
Eurotalk Ltd, 315 New Kings Rd.,London SW64RF, UK.
email: 100442.1701@compuserve.com

Údarás na Gaeltachta

Údarás na Gaeltachta, the Gaeltacht Authority, is the regional government agency with responsibility for the Economic, Social and Language/Cultural development of the Gaeltacht (Irish speaking) areas of Ireland. Údarás na Gaeltachta has a 13 member board, seven of whom are directly elected by the people of the Gaeltacht while the remaining six, including the Chairman, are appointed by the Minister responsible for the Gaeltacht. The Gaeltacht areas are located mainly along the Western and South-Western seaboards. They cover substantial coastal and inland parts of counties Donegal, Mayo, Galway and Kerry as well as smaller parts of counties Waterford and Meath. The Gaeltacht off-shore Islands are Tory and Aranmore (Donegal), Achill (Mayo), the three Aran Islands of Inis Mor, Inis Meam and Inis Oirr (Galway) and Cape Clear (Cork).

An tÚdarás pursues its core language preservation and development objectives through job and wealth creation strategies and initiatives.

Údarás na Gaeltachta carries out its role in a variety of ways, including the provision of professional advice as well as financial assistance to new enterprise. In partnership with local communities, and in keeping with its language and cultural development brief, An tÚdarás plays an active role in a broad range of initiatives, from Irish Language pre- schools, youth Clubs, local festivals, community arts, sporting and other community events. The over-riding objective is the preservation and extension of Irish as an everyday community language.

As a Regional Development Authority, Údarás na Gaeltachta actively promotes an integrated approach to Gaeltacht development through a combination of direct-action programmes, partnerships with voluntary and community-based organisations and facilitating the sourcing and implementation of European Union programmes and funding.

GaelSaoire

A recent strategic initiative is the development and promotion of Cultural Tourism. The Authority's objective is to brand and promote the Gaeltacht areas as very different holiday destinations, because of the Irish language, spoken as a community language, and because of the overall distinct culture and ethos of the Gaeltacht, reflected in its music, song and dance in areas naturally endowed with some of Ireland's finest scenery. This tourism initiative will be pursued through the effective use and promotion of the brand name GaelSaoire, holidays in the Gaeltacht.
GaelSaoire is working in tandem with community based Co-operatives, Tourism Committees and Development Associations throughout the Gaeltacht to identify the tourism resource and marketable potential of each area. Working with and through these community groups, GaelSaoire is supporting worthwhile cultural tourism product development and joint marketing initiatives that will portray the Gaeltacht as a quality holiday destination that is distinct and offering an emotional experience of Ireland that differs from other parts of the country. Conscious of the valuable multiplier effect of visitor spending in the community GaelSaoire will help to develop suitable flagship holiday facilities in strategic areas throughout the Gaeltacht and in partnership with the Gaeltacht communities.

Údarás na Gaeltachta's Headoffice is at
Na Forbacha, Galway (Tel: 091 503100).

Regional Offices are in An Bun Beag (Bunbeg) Co. Donegal (Tel. 075 60100),
An Daingean (Dingle), Co.Kerry (Tel; 066 50100),
Béal an Mhuirthead (Belmullet), Co.Mayo (Tel; 097 81418),
Baile Mhic Íre (Ballymakeera), Co. Cork (Tel: 02645423).

GaelSaoire *can be contacted at*
Freephone 1800-621-600

Údarás na Gaeltachta

Fold out map of the Gaeltacht regions
inside back cover.

Irish Language Ireland
is part of the series

FACT PACK

guides to all aspects of Ireland,
both of local and tourism interest.
A full list is available from the publishers
(*send sae*)
MORRIGAN, KILLALA, CO.MAYO

Morrigan Books is part of Morigna MediaCo Teoranta,
publishers on the internet of

ATLANTIC ISLAND

http://www.atlanticisland.ie

1 Dún na nGall

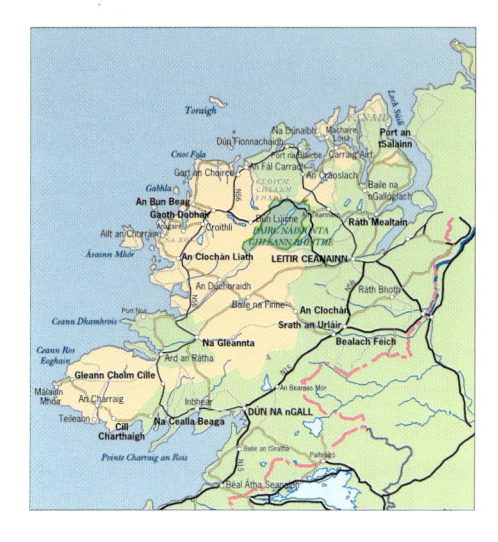

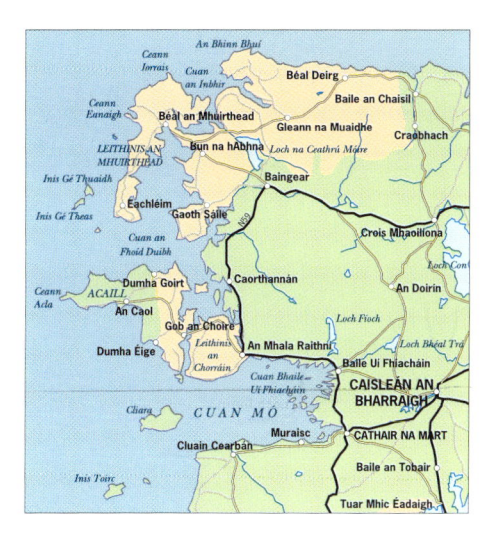

2 Maigh Eo

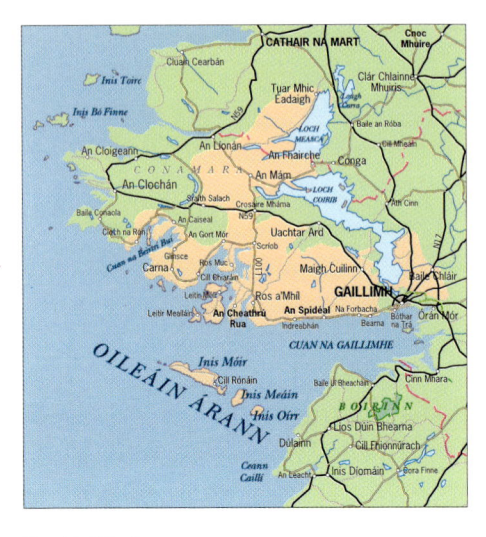

3 Gaillimh

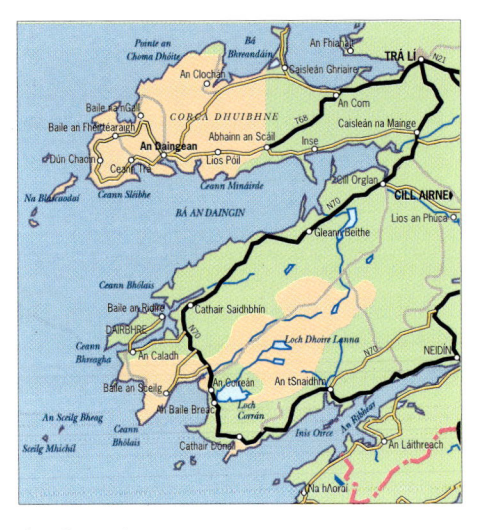

4 Ciarraí

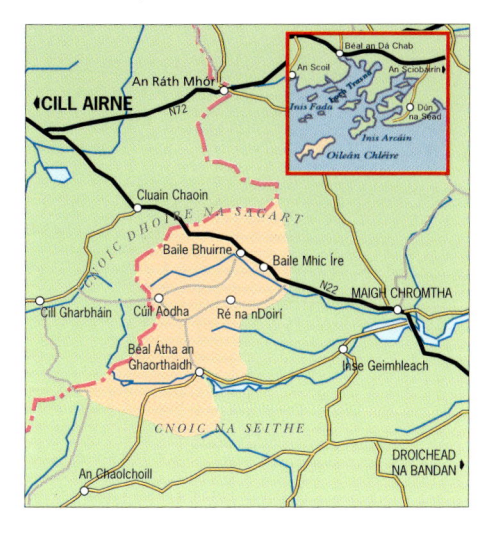

5 Corcaigh

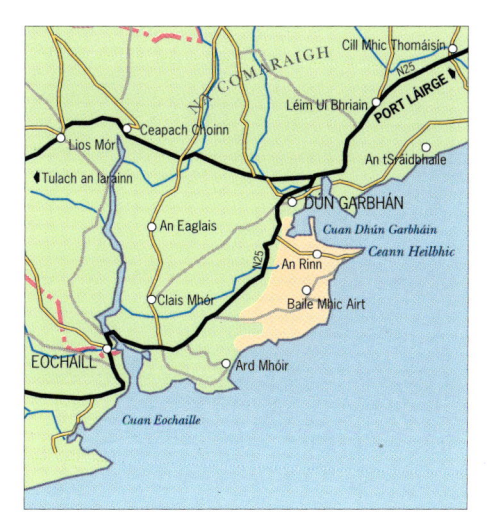

6 Port Láirge

Doire *(Derry)*

Latharna *(Larne)*

Béal Feirste *(Belfast)*

Muineachán *(Monaghan)*

Dún Dealgan *(Dundalk)*

Longfort *(Longford)*

Ceanannas *(Kells)*

7

An Uaimh *(Navan)*

AN MHÍ

Baile Átha Cliath *(Dublin)*

Dún Laoghaire

Port Laoise

Ceatharlach *(Carlow)*

Cill Chainnigh *(Kilkenny)*

Loch Garman *(Wexford)*

Ros Láir *(Rosslare)*

PORT LÁIRGE

Port Láirge *(Waterford)*

Dún Garbhán *(Dungarvan)*

Eochaill *(Youghal)*

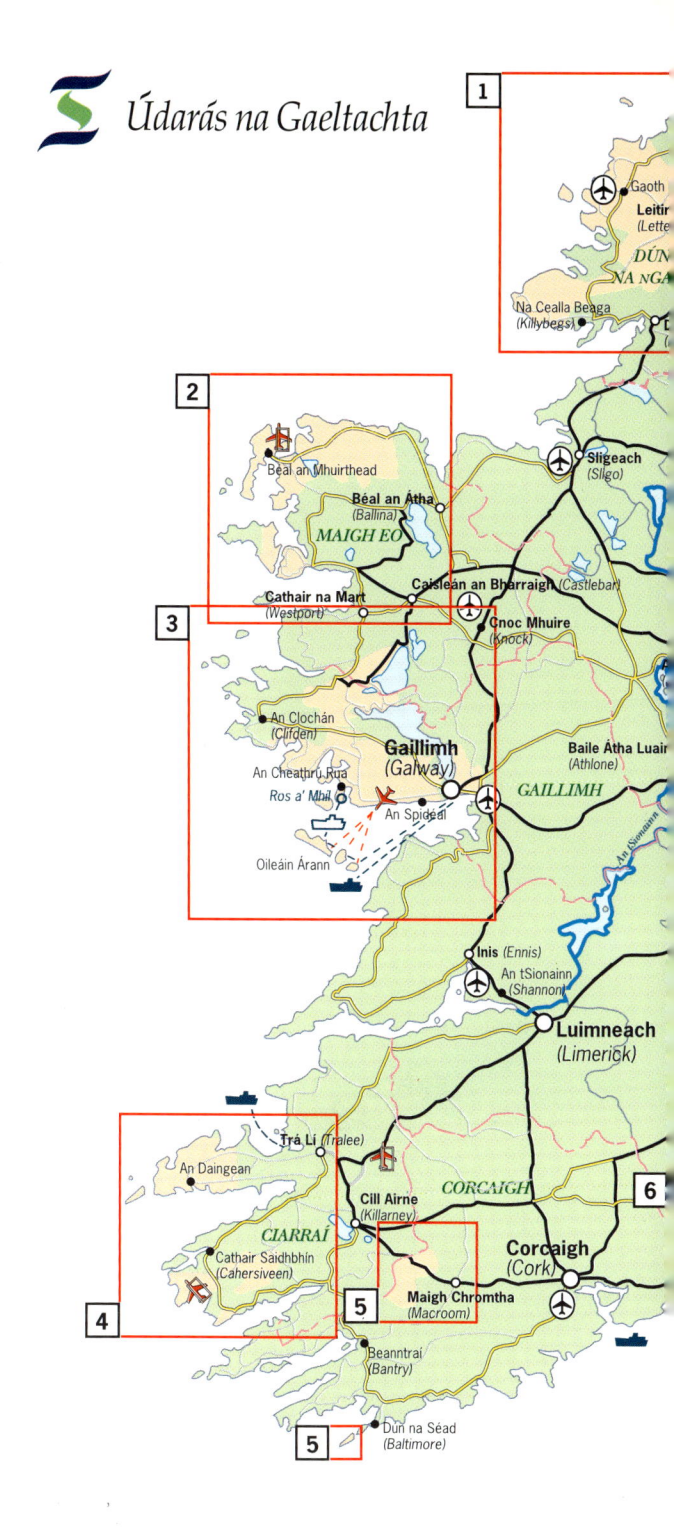

Údarás na Gaeltachta

- **1** Gaoth Dobhair, Leitir Ceanainn (Letterkenny)
- Na Cealla Beaga (Killybegs)
- DÚN NA nGALL

- **2** Béal an Mhuirthead
- Béal an Átha (Ballina)
- MAIGH EO
- Cathair na Mart (Westport)
- Caisleán an Bharraigh (Castlebar)
- Cnoc Mhuire (Knock)
- Sligeach (Sligo)

- **3** An Clochán (Clifden)
- An Cheathrú Rua
- Ros a' Mhíl
- An Spidéal
- Gaillimh (Galway)
- Oileáin Árann
- Baile Átha Luain (Athlone)
- GAILLIMH

- Inis (Ennis)
- An tSionainn (Shannon)
- Luimneach (Limerick)

- **4** Trá Lí (Tralee)
- An Daingean
- Cathair Saidhbhín (Cahersiveen)
- CIARRAÍ
- Cill Airne (Killarney)
- **5** Maigh Chromtha (Macroom)
- CORCAIGH
- Corcaigh (Cork)
- Beanntraí (Bantry)
- **5** Dún na Séad (Baltimore)
- **6**

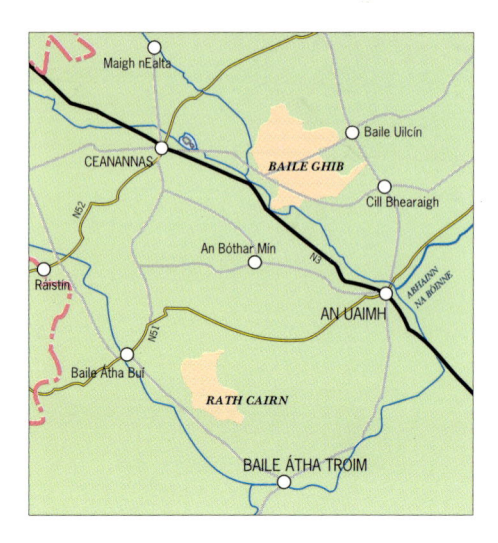

7 An Mhí

▬▬▬	Príomh Bhealaí Náisiúnta
▬▬▬	Fobhóithre/Bealaí Eile
───	Bealaí Treasach
▬▬▬	Teorainn Chontae
─·─·─	Teorainn Contaetha Gaeltachta
▆	Gaeltachtaí
▬▬▬	Aibhneacha
✈	Aerfoirt Idirnáisiúnta
✈	Aerfoirt Réigiúnacha/Aerstráice
🚢	Calafort Trádálach/Báid Farantóireachta Ghluaisteán
⛴	Báid Farantóireachta Phaisinéirí

Eochair